Great Ideas for
Bathrooms

Great Ideas for
Bathrooms

Bath · ew York · Singapore · Hong Kong · Coogne · Dehi · Mebourne

This is a Parragon Publishing Book

Copyright © Parragon Books Ltd 2009

Parragon Books Ltd
Queen Street House
4, Queen Street
Bath, BA1 1HE
United Kingdom

Original text: Cristian Campos
Concept: Mireia Casanovas Soley
Design: Emma Termes Parera

Copyright © 2009 Parragon Books Ltd
for the English edition

English edition produced by: APE International, Richmond, VA
Translation from German: Dr. Maureen Basedow for APE International

ISBN: 978-1-4075-5273-6

Printed in China

Introduction

Planning

Next to the kitchen, the bathroom is probably the most frequently used room in the home. Its location, form, and appearance are always given special attention. If you want to build a house, one of your first decisions is where to put the bathrooms, since the necessary pipes and drains need to be in place from the very beginning of construction. The next decision is whether or not the bathroom should have natural light. In a small apartment, there is often very little choice.

Design questions come next. Which color scheme should you choose so that the bathroom fits in well with the rest of the house? Will you need extra ventilation to keep humidity under control? Do you want a shower, or a bathtub, or both? Would you like to have a bidet? How many sinks do you need? What kind of heating system works best? Would you prefer built-in cabinets or freestanding storage units? Do you want a unified decorative scheme? What about lighting?

In principle, every bathroom is made up of three separate areas: the sink, with its associated countertops, shelves, cabinets, and towel holders; the so-called "wet zone," consisting of the shower and bathtub; and finally the hygienic area, which includes the toilet and sometimes a bidet. The

Design: Marco Savorelli
Photography: © Matteo Piazza

first two areas are relatively uncomplicated and can be located anywhere. The toilet and bidet, however, must be located near the waste pipe. There are a number of ways to separate the three areas. Solid partition walls provide complete, physical separation. Visual distinctions can be made by varying the wall color, floor covering, or materials. More often, bathroom decor is stylistically integrated throughout, with each area transitioning seamlessly into the next.

Size plays a role. The planning for a 100 square foot (20 m²) bathroom is very different from what is required to lay out an apartment bathroom that might be less than half that size. A bidet is probably not an option for a very small space, and a shower becomes much more practical than a bathtub. Wall-hung toilets or sinks can also save room. Decorative choices and lighting effects can be as important as layout in making a small space seem larger.

Design: Himmel Haus, Andrea Held
Photography: © Nacása & Partners

Design: Archikubik
Photography: © Eugeni Pons

Furnishing

Every piece of furniture in your bathroom should serve one primary goal: organization. Personal care items such as towels, bathrobes, soap, shower gel, shampoo, toilet paper, hair dryers, and medications need to be both accessible and protected from moisture. Most bathroom storage is located near the sink, where most of these items will be used. Some, such as toilet paper holders, may be found closer to the hygienic area if the space allows it.

It is important to remember that not every piece of furniture is suitable for a bathroom. Shelving made of unfinished wood should not be used anywhere near the wet zone. Waterproof materials are by far the best choice. Stylish, modular systems made of metal can also be used.

The lack of space in the average bathroom presents the greatest challenge. Many bathrooms are not only small, but narrow as well. Happily, there are a number of design solutions that address just this situation. Sliding doors on cabinets are recommended, as are shelves or small wall cabinets that take advantage of every corner of the room. Cabinets and corner shelves are the best choice for the small items that accumulate over time in a bathroom. Storage units on rollers are another option.

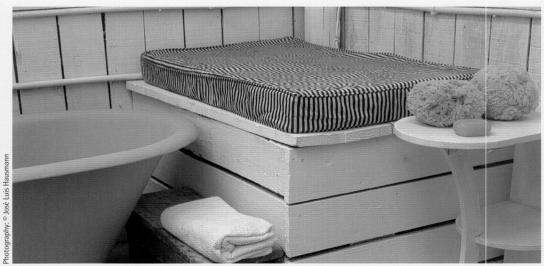

Towels can be hung in myriad ways. Simple hooks on the back of a door, or mounted on the wall behind it, make use of what is often wasted space. Bathroom furnishings come in a wealth of different materials, including finished wood, aluminum, glass, and stainless steel. Style options run from rustic and baroque through minimalist and modern.

When designing a bathroom, practical considerations often come first, but this does not mean that you cannot express your personal style here just as in any other part of your house or apartment. A bathroom does not have to be unattractive, and it should harmonize with the style of the rest of your home.

Photography: © Eugeni Pons

Photography: © José Luis Hausmann

Walls and Floors

Walls and all the other surfaces in your bathroom should be waterproof. Moisture-resistant bathroom rugs are available in a large variety of colors, shapes, sizes, and patterns. Choose a designer rug and let your imagination run wild! Tile flooring is most common in the wet zone, especially in front of the bathtub or shower. Larger, glazed ceramic tiles can provide attractive decorative accents.

Interior decorators and architects are increasingly using wood with high oil content for bathroom walls and floors, even in the wet zone. Wood is easily adapted to almost any style. Tropical hardwoods are especially popular, but think before you buy! Many tropical hardwoods are endangered. Locally grown oak, birch, and cedar work just as well, and can be harvested in a more ecologically sound manner.

Marble is another popular material. This elegant stone often comes across as somewhat cool, and generally it should be used in combination with warmer materials. The great advantage of marble is its utter impermeability to moisture.

Photography: © Eugeni Pons

Architect: Roy Leone Design Studio   Photography: © Edouard Huber/Archphoto

For walls, waterproof or moisture-resistant wallpapers and paints should be used in the splash zone around sinks and hygienic fixtures. For areas in direct contact with running water, tile is the better option.

In recent years, materials that had only rarely been used in bathrooms have gained in popularity, including concrete, stone, metal, and plastic. Used judiciously, these less common materials can transform your bath into a personal wellness oasis enhanced by your own unique style.

Photography: © Ricardo Labougle

Design: Ana Peña
Photography: © J. J. Pérez Iscla

Color

Color creates atmosphere within a space, making both a personal and a stylistic statement. The colors of a room are the greatest factor influencing how it feels to be inside it. Light colors, especially natural white, make a bathroom feel bright and expansive: contours recede and the walls seem to shimmer in the distance. The very corners of the room are softened when the walls are white. Dark colors, by contrast, make a bathroom feel smaller and cozier. They are best reserved for large bathrooms or as contrasting accents.

Orange, yellow, and red are warm colors. Blue and purple tones are cooler, and greens should be used with caution. Combined with the fluorescent lighting used in most bathrooms, too much green drains the ambient light from a space, swallowing up the other colors.

White remains the color of choice for a lot of bathrooms. It makes what is often a physically small room seem larger, and can be easily combined with other colors. Glossy or matte white creates an impression of freshness and purity; and the softer blue tones work similarly.

Photography: © Jeff Heatley

Photography: © Eugeni Pons

In the end, the choice of colors is highly individual and very much a matter of personal taste. As long as you (and the people living with you) like the colors, there are few limits. Unconventional color combinations can create a bathroom that exudes style and originality. To draw attention to a brightly colored decorative element or wall treatment in the middle your bathroom, paint the rest of the room in complementary, neutral colors for emphasis.

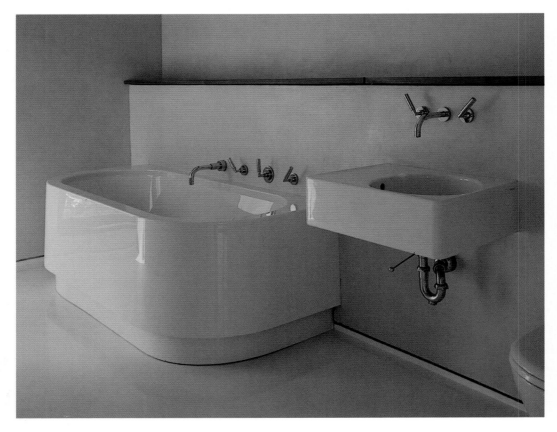

Light

As is the case in other rooms in your home, daylight provides ideal illumination for your bathroom. While a house is still in the planning stages, the bathroom should be located so that natural light can enter through a window or skylight, either of which can also be used for extra ventilation. Blinds and curtains can be used to shield the interior of the bath from view, but should be made of the thinnest materials possible to maximize the daylight that can enter.

There are a number of choices when it comes to artificial lighting for your bathroom. Purely decorative lamps are not recommended. While these may be attractive to look at, they don't provide enough illumination on their own. Bathrooms need a primary source of warm light capable of brightening up every corner without being blinding. Halogen lamps or even entire halogen lighting systems work particularly well; additional lighting can be added to focus on specific areas of the room. Adjustable track lighting, for example, can provide extra light for shaving or grooming. Spotlights might be positioned on either side of a mirror over a sink, or built into a makeup mirror. All light fixtures should be splash resistant and installed according to current guidelines regarding safe distance from running water. Another option is to illuminate bathroom fixtures

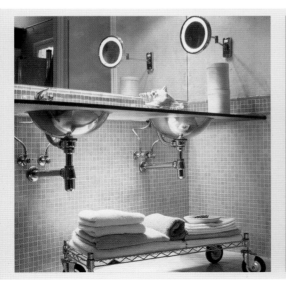 

themselves from within. Bathtubs can be enhanced with "underwater" lighting, and bulbs set within a glass washstand can illuminate the bathroom sink from below. It goes without saying that any lighting in this category must be completely waterproof!

Additional decorative lighting effects also have their place. Colored light bulbs and neon lights can also create exciting color accents in your bathroom.

Design: Duravit

Halogen lamps on the ceiling fill every corner of the bathroom with light.

The long rectangular mirror works well within this small narrow bathroom.

Built-in shelves instead of cabinets make the best use of limited space while giving this bathroom its own unique look.

This heater warms not only the room, but also the towels hung on it.

Suspended sinks are space-savers in very small bathrooms.

Design: Guita Maleki & Pascal Cheikh Djavadi
Photography: © Chris Gascoigne/View

Kinds of
Bathrooms

Classic Bathrooms

In most houses and apartments, bathrooms are enclosed spaces with four walls and a door. This doesn't mean that the "typical" bathroom inside has to be boring. This chapter includes a wealth of options for creative bathroom design. Unique arrangements of decorative elements such as gliding panels, transparent partitions, built-in furniture, high-tech materials, and freestanding shower cubicles are guaranteed to impress.

The bathrooms in this section were originally designed for unique planning situations including a renovated attic, an apartment with an unusual layout, and a very small living space. They can also be adapted for other situations. If you want a bathroom like no other, have a look at these for inspiration. Your fantasy can become reality!

Architect: Desai/Chia Studio
Photography: © Joshua McHugh

 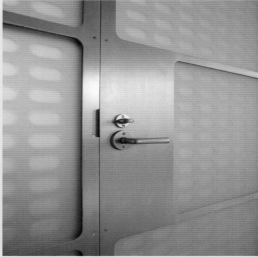

Architect: Eichinger or Knechtel Photography: © Margherita Spiluttini

Photography: © Markus Tomaselli Rataplan

Photography: © Markus Tomaselli Rataplan

Architect: Eichinger or Knechtel Photography: © Margherita Spiluttini

Architect: Manel Torres/In Disseny Photography: © Stephan Zahring

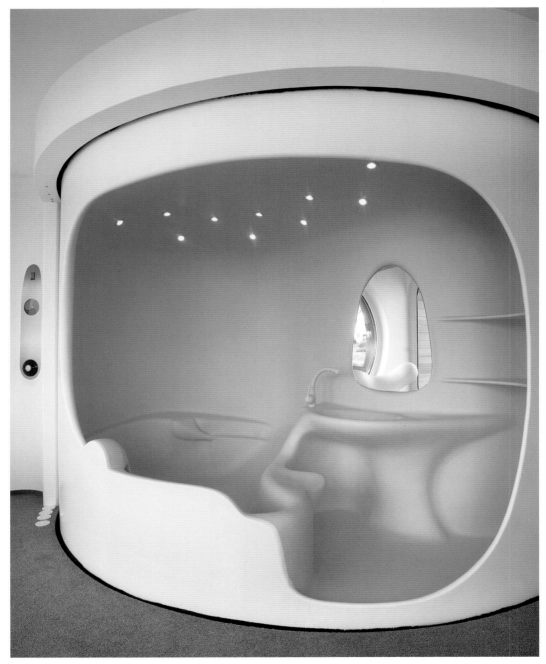

Architect: Luigi Colani, Hanse Haus   Photography: © Hanse Haus

Architect: Splitterwerk   Photography: © Paul Ott

Architect: Dorotea Oliva Photography: © Virginia del Giudice

Architect: Holzer Klober Architekturen   Photography: © Simone Rosenberg

Architect: Fokkema Architechten Photography: © Christian Richters

Architect: Fokkema Architechten Photography: © Christian Richters

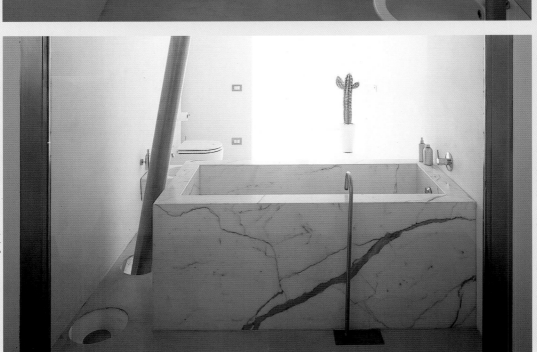

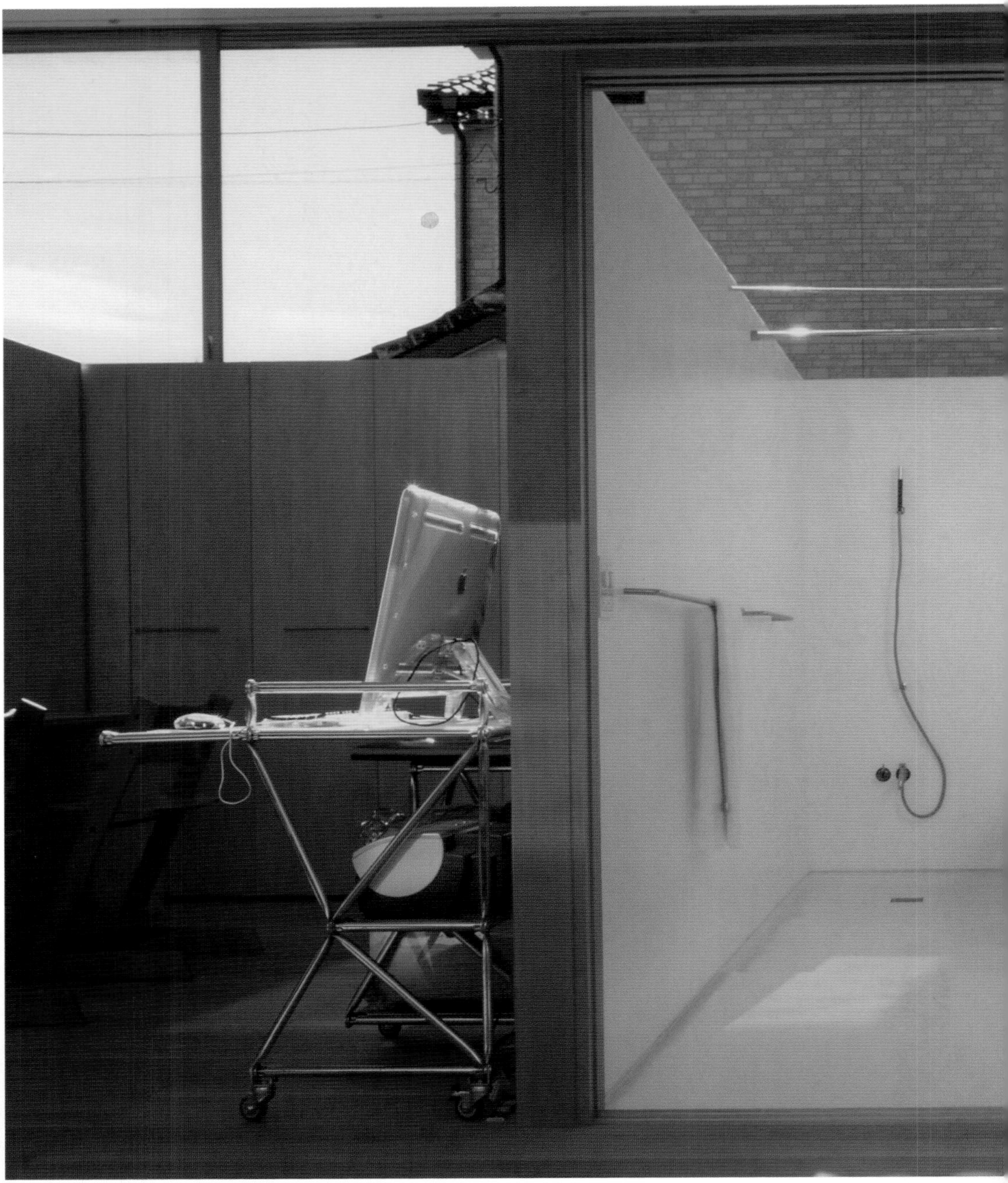

Photography: © Katsuhida Kida Photography

Architect: Takaharu & Yui Tezuka/Tezuka Arquitectos, Masahiro Ikeda/Mias

Architect: Nancy Robbins & Blau-Centre de la Llar Photography: © José Luis Hausmann

Architect: Nancy Robbins & Blau-Centre de la Llar Photography: © José Luis Hausmann

Architect: Luca Mercatelli Photography: © Matteo Piazza

Architect: Luca Mercatelli Photography: © Matteo Piazza

Architect: Hugh Broughton Photography: © Carlos Dominguez

Open-Plan Bathrooms

In addition to the classic, enclosed bathrooms, there are also open-plan variations in which specific elements—most often the bathtub—are not hidden behind walls, but are instead fully integrated into the living space. Indeed, there are incredibly beautiful bathtubs that are simply too wonderful to hide away. Take a look around and see what you find!

Most open-plan designs are found in apartments inhabited by couples or singles, or in houses where the transition between public and private space is not strictly defined. These cutting edge designs have little in common with traditional bathrooms. Some open plan bathrooms, for example, have no concealing walls or partitions whatsoever. Others might be described as hybrid plans that separate the more intimate zones with low partitions and glass walls. The advantages of open-plan bathrooms are many: they make optimal use of available space, are easy to access, and enjoy unobstructed light. With an open-plan bathroom, your imagination quite literally has no boundaries.

Architect: Peter Tyberghien Photography: © Alejandro Bahamón

Architect: Anne Bugagnani & Diego Fortunato Photography: © Eugeni Pons

Architect: Anne Bugagnani & Diego Fortunato Photography: © Eugeni Pons

Architect: Paula Pryke Photography: © Wayne Vincent/Red Cover

Architect: Yamaoka Design Studio Photography: © Nacása & Partners

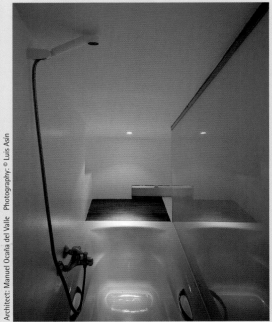

Architect: Blockarquitecture Photography: © Chris Tubbs

Integrated bathrooms

Bathrooms that are directly accessible from a bedroom are often called "en suite," a term borrowed from the French. Designers refer to these as integrated bathrooms because they are fully integrated into the plan of the bedroom. They are not considered stand-alone facilities, but rather part of the bedroom layout and design. In many instances, it is difficult to say where the bedroom ends and the bathroom begins. In other cases, the bathroom's placement and design follows the classic model, and is physically separated from the bedroom by a door.

The possibilities for creative integration of the two spaces are nearly unlimited. The original plan of the bedroom is a factor, as is the degree of privacy desired. Light sources, placement of drains, and ventilation also need to be taken into consideration. Most importantly, care must be taken to ensure that the humidity generated in a bathroom doesn't damage clothing or other items stored in the bedroom. A sliding glass door between the two rooms is usually sufficient to prevent this.

Architect: Guillaume Dreyfuss Photography: © Kurt Arrigo

Architect: Hugh Broughton Photography: © Carlos Domínguez

Architect: Deu i Deu Photography: © José Luis Hausmann

Architect: Deu i Deu Photography: © José Luis Hausmann

Architect: Deu i Deu Photography: © José Luis Hausmann

Architect: Pler Arquitectos Photography: © Jose Luis Hausmann

Architect: Pler Arquitectos Photography: © Jose Luis Hausmann

Architect: Jorges Villon Photography: © Andreas von Einsiedel/Red Cover

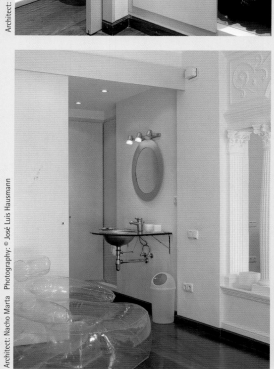

Architect: Pablo Chiaporri Photography: © Virginia del Guidice

A unified light source that illuminates every corner and angle of the bathroom equally eliminates the need for separate light fixtures.

Using tiles of identical size for the floor and the walls makes the bathroom appear more cohesive.

A glass partition protects wooden cabinets from water splashed from the bathtub.

Glass partitions filter light and help create the impression of more space.

If there is enough room, a stand-alone shower is an attractive option.

Architect: Guita Maleki & Pascal Cheikh Djavadi
Photography: © Solvi do Santos/Omnia

Fixtures

Bathtubs

When selecting a bathtub, you will have an unbelievable range of shapes and sizes to choose from. There is really something for everyone, from nostalgic claw-footed bathtubs reminiscent of days gone by to the high-tech variety with integrated hydromassage and steam bath functions. The standard bathtub size is 5 feet long and between 30 and 32 inches wide. In addition you will find everything from smaller square tubs, not uncommon and mainly for sitting and therapeutic soaking, to enormous tubs approaching the size of small swimming pools, and many in between.

In principle, no bathroom is too small for a bathtub. Most are ceramic, although plastics such as acrylic and metacrylate are increasingly widespread. Designer bathtubs can be made of iron and steel. Large whirlpool baths with hydromassage, though expensive, offer every imaginable comfort. The massage jets can be adjusted with a control panel like any other home appliance.

Design: Naomi Cleaver
Photography: © Ed Reeve/Red Cover

Architect: Héctor Restrepo Calvo, Heres Arquitectura   Photography: © Nuria Fuentes

Photography: © Nuria Fuentes

Bathtub: Acquagrande by Flaminia

Design: Greek   Photography: © Nuria Fuentes

Bathtub: Acquagrande by Flaminia

Architect: John Pawson   Photography: © Ken Hayden/Red Cover

Photography: © James Mitchell/Red Cover

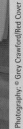

Architect: Alex Meitlis Architecture and Design Photography: © Yael Pincus

Photography: © Andreas von Einsiedel/Red Cover

Design: Paio by Duravit

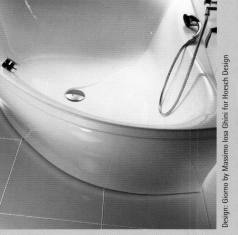

Design: Giorno by Massimo Iosa Ghini for Hoesch Design

Design: Daro for Duravit

Design: Norman Foster for Hoesch Design

Design: Norman Foster for Hoesch Design

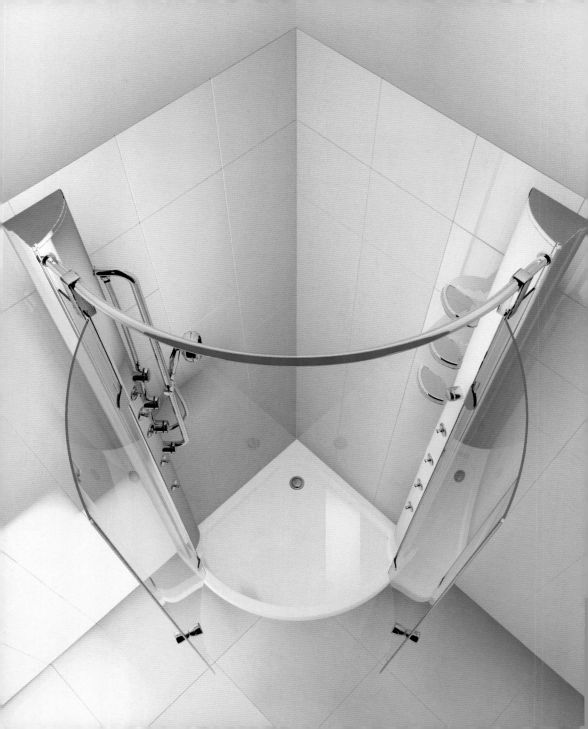

Showers

While the size of your bathroom may determine whether or not you can have a bathtub, almost any space can accommodate a shower. The smallest can fit into little more than 2 square feet (60 cm²). If the space was any smaller than that it would be impossible to move or turn around! The larger the shower, the more comfortable your bathing experience will be.

Shower bases can be square, rectangular, round, or angled and may be constructed of ceramic, wood, marble, plastic, or fiberglass. Some come with plastic folding seats, which are particularly useful for the elderly. Other showers are so simple that they consist of little more than a drain and a showerhead attached to a hose. A shower curtain or glass door protects the rest of the bathroom from splashing water and minimizes the effect of condensation. Showers that are completely enclosed by watertight materials may offer steam bath and massage options. If you have a large bathroom, design options for your shower are nearly endless.

Photography: © Reiner Lautwein

Birmingham Showerhead by Ann Sacks

Design: Deu i Deu Styling: Ana Profitós

Design: Augusto Le Monnier Interior design: Lorna Agusti, Natalie G. Novelles

Design: Hüffer Ramin Photography: © Werner Huthmacher

Design: Sol y luna by Bardelli

Sinks

It is not difficult to find a sink: most specialty stores offer an extensive selection, making it easy to find one that meets your needs and design expectations. Do you prefer a round sink, a square one, or a rectangular, oval, or freeform design? As long as the sink is practical and functional, any shape or style is possible. Materials include ceramic, wood, plastic, glass, stainless steel, and combinations of these. The standard minimum diameter for the basin of a bathroom sink is just 1 foot (30 cm). If it is any smaller, hand washing becomes difficult. You can choose a striking stand-alone sink or build the sink into a complete bathroom system that visually unifies all the fixtures: sink, toilet, bidet, shower, and bathtub. Both options have advantages.

Older sinks usually stood on a high foot or broad pedestal. Today, sinks are more commonly mounted on the wall. This creates additional storage space beneath the basin for hand towel racks and cabinets. When instal-ling a bathroom sink, take care that there is enough space between the basin and the taps. If they are too close, water will splash everywhere. Many sinks include built in slots and depressions for soap and other bathroom accessories, such as toothpaste and toothbrushes. Shelving underneath a sink can be both practical and decorative.

Design: Terra by Puntmobles Photography: © Llum Nacho Pérez

Design: Neo for Sanico

Design: Vero by Duravit

Design: Flaminia

Design: Moon by Sanico Photography: © Roberto Constantini

Design: Philippe Starck for Duravit

Design: 'Waterblade by Peter Jamieson for Ritmonio

Design: Play by Althea Ceramica Photography: © Roberto Constantini

Design: Boing by Puntmobles Photography: © Terra de Llum Nacho Pérez

Design: Elle by Althea Ceramica Photography: © Roberto Constantini

Design: Neo by Sanico

Design: Elle by Althea Ceramica Photography: © Roberto Constantini

Design: Bucket Sink by Alape

Design: Oneday by Permesso

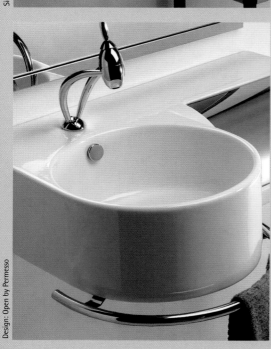

Design: Open by Permesso

Design: Rotondo by Permesso

Design: Sistema Glass by Ludovica and Roberto Palomba for Permesso

Sieger Design by Alape

Toilets and Bidets

As is true for other bathroom fixtures, today there is a wide array of design options for toilets and bidets. Once dull and purely functional, these essential fixtures are now available in myriad styles, shapes, materials, colors, and sizes. Stylish toilet and bidet sets lend visual unity to the hygienic zone. Individual pieces that stand out within a bathroom are also a good choice.

Toilets and bidets are nearly always made of ceramic, although stainless steel is gaining in popularity. Until recently, nearly all toilets and bidets stood on pedestal bases. Today, they are more likely to be wall-mounted, with the water tank concealed within the wall. Standing toilets with the water tank inside the base are also popular. While the hanging models are a good solution for small bathrooms, they can be difficult to install, requiring the attention of an expert plumber. The distance between a toilet and bidet should be at least 10 inches (25 cm).

Design: A Prima Photography: © Nuria Fuentes

Design: Flaminia

Design: Flaminia

Design: Ana Simó Photography: © Nuria Fuentes

Design: Stephen Varady Architecture Photography: © Stephen Varady

Design: Flaminia

Design: Flaminia

Fittings and Accessories

If you want to give your bathroom your own personal touch, fittings such as faucets, showerheads, and handles should not be ignored. There are a number of beautiful designer sets for sinks, showers, and bathtubs that help visually unify the space. Most faucets today are designed so that hot and cold water flows out of a single spout. Older designs like the swan neck are still popular, though, and most faucets are still turned on and off either with levers or twist grip handles. Double-spouted faucets are available, although these are less practical for warm water. Many sink fittings incorporate hand towel warmers—who doesn't appreciate a warm hand towel? Accessories found near the sink include soap dispensers, soap dishes, toilet paper holders, and a bathroom mirror, sometimes with a medicine cabinet behind it.

Materials run from plastic and metal to ceramic, wood, and stone. Fittings can be enhanced by lacquer, glaze, chrome, or gilding. Designs ranging from avant-garde to traditional are available to give each bathroom its own personal style, just like the rest of your home.

Design: Habana by Sanico

Open Mueble by Sanico

Open Mueble by Sanico

Fogo by Duravit

Tango by Sanico

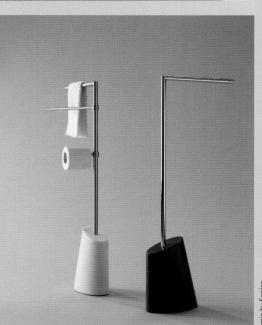

Fermin by Sanico

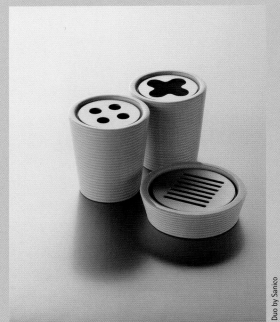

Equis by Sanico

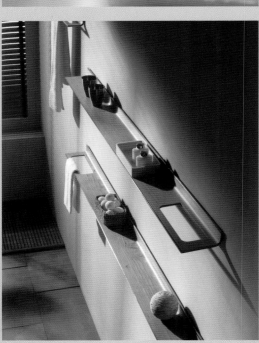

Fixtures by Permesso

Radio Collection by Struch

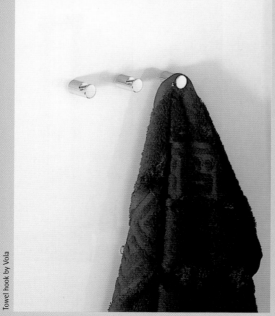

Towel hook by Vola

Design: Glòria Duran Torrellas   Photography: © Nuria Fuentes

Photography: © José Luis Hausmann

Diametrotrentacinque by Davide Vercelli for Ritmonio

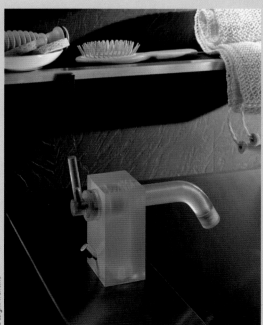

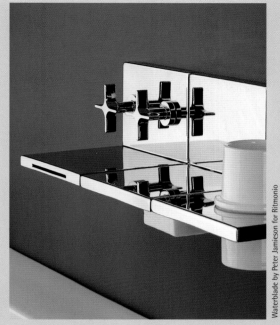

Diametrotrentacinque by Davide Vercelli for Ritmonio

Waterblade by Peter Jamieson for Ritmonio

Design: Trentino

Design: Trentino

Layout

Making the Most of Your Space

Even the smallest of bathrooms can be enhanced by a creative layout. Wall-mounted toilets take up less space than the pedestal kind. Installing the water tank inside the wall saves still more room. A hanging sink, or one mounted on a slender metal stand, creates space underneath for hand towel racks and other storage. Built-in shelving and cabinets are another popular choice. When laying out your bathroom, make sure you are not blocking any light sources. A brightly lit bathroom seems larger than a dim, shadowy space. Use glass partitions that let light flow in and large mirrors to reflect both direct and ambient light around the room. Bright and uniformly lighting and the limited use of tile—better to confine it to small areas rather than covering the entire floor or wall with it—create the illusion of a larger space.

The larger your bathroom window, the better. Curtains, shades, and blinds should be made of lightweight materials in pale colors that block the view without blocking natural light. The walls, floors, and furnishings should be predominantly light, in colors such as white or pale yellow. These colors reflect light better than darker, deeper tones, making your bathroom look and feel airier and larger. If you like, choose an individual element as a focal point for the room. It is important that all the other fixtures in the bathroom work well with the more vivid design pieces.

Architect: Cho Slade
Photography: © Jordi Miralles

Architect: John Butterworth Photography: © Paul Warchol

Consider whether you might want to do without a bathtub and instead build in a comfortable shower. In very small bathrooms, a bidet would also be obtrusive. Finally, you can also counter the limitations of a small room and create the impression of space through your choice of materials. Glass and steel, for example, generally occupy less space than similar fixtures in wood, and they also give the visual impression of expansiveness.

Photography: © José Luis Hausmann

Architect: Francesca Donati Studio Photography: © Andrea Martiradonna

Architect: Hiroaki Ohtani Photography: © Kouji Okamoto

Architect: Studio Associato Bettinelli Photography: © Andrea Martiradonna

Architect: Cloud 9 Photography: © Luis Ros

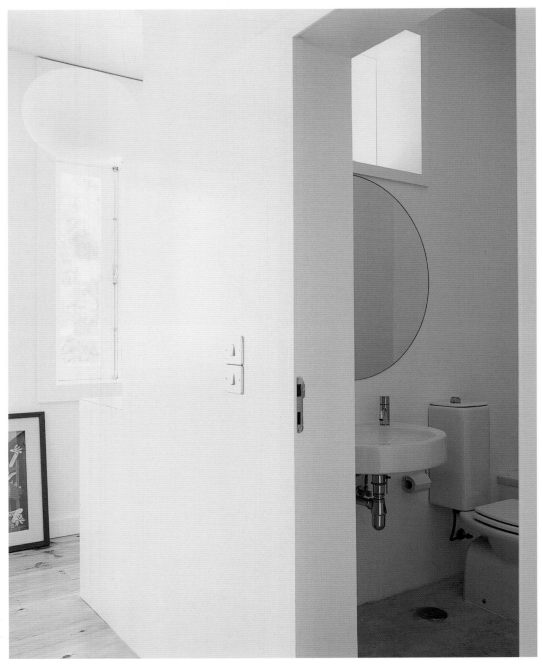

Architect: Inês Lobo   Photography: © Sergio Mah

Architect: Shonda Warner Photography: © Andreas von Einsiedel/Red Cover

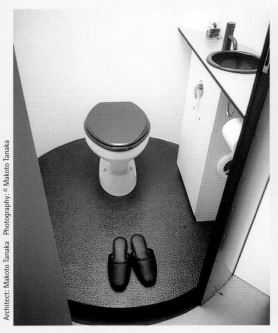

Architect: BEHF Architekten Photography: © Rupert Steiner

Architect: Massimo d'Alessandro & Associati Photography: © Andrea Martiradonna

Architect: Francesc Rifé Photography: © Sandro Garofalo

Architect: Stone Designs Photography: © Juan Merinero

Domani, by Sieger Design for Dornbracht

Design: Marisa Garcia & Alex Baeza   Photography: © José Luis Hausmann

Design: Randy Brown Arquitectos   Photography: © Farshid Assassi

Design: Philippe Starck   Photography: © Jordi Miralles

Architect: Drewes & Strenge Architekten Photography: © Christian Richters

Interior design: René Dekker Photography: © James Silverman

Design: Jo Crepain Arquitectos Photography: © Jan Verlinde, Ludo Noël

Design: PMG Arquitectos, Peter Grumpel, Jury Álvarez Photography: © Pep Escoda

Design: Michael Carapetian Photography: © Andrea Martiradonna

Design: Jennifer Randall & Associates Photography: © Werner Huthmacher

Photography: © Jordi Miralles

i29 Office for Spatial Design Photography: © Jeroen Dellensen

Design: Holger Kleine Photography: © Alexander von Reiswitz, Frank Seehausen

Photography: © Jordi Sarrà

Architect: Splitterwerk Photography: © Paul Ott

Architect: Manuel Serrano Arquitectos Photography: © J. Latova

Design: Holger Kleine Photography: © Werner Huthmacher

Design: Pipe Dreams Photography: © Carlos Domínguez

Design: Pablo Uribe Photography: © Pep Escoda

Design: Simon Conder Photography: © Maite Gallardo

Architect: Raphaël Orts, Nicolas Balleriaux Photography: © Laurent Brandajs

Architect: Luca Rolla Photography: © Andrea Martiradonna

Architect: Joan Pons Forment Photography: © Eugeni Pons

Architect: Mutsue Hayakusa/Cell Space Arquitectos Photography: © Satoshi Asakawa

Architect: Anima Photography: © Paul Rivera

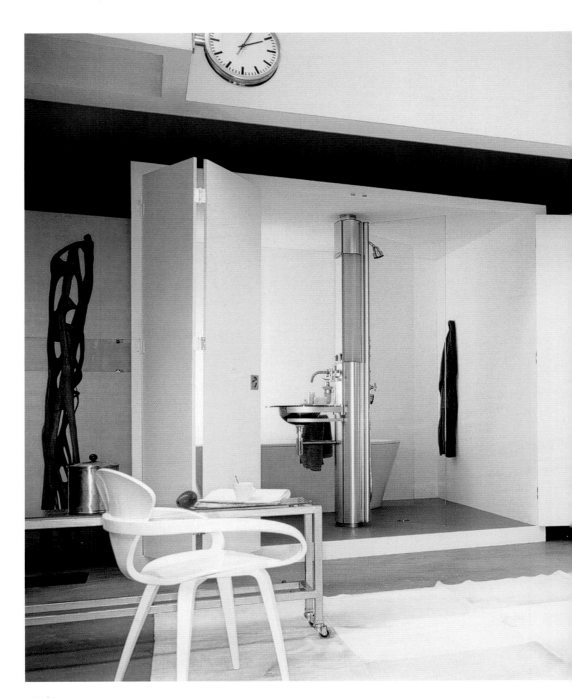

Architect: Feyferlik-Fritzer Photography: © Paul Ott

Architect: Héctor Restrepo Calvo, Heres Arquitectura Photography: © Nuria Fuentes

Architect: Schappacher White Photography: © Steve Schappacher & Rhea White

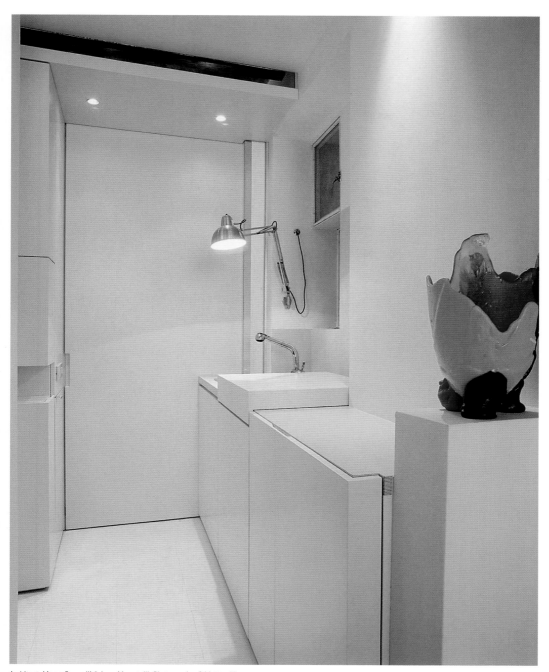

Architect: Marco Savorelli & Luca Mercatelli Photography: © Matteo Piazza

Large mirrors emphasize the impression of space and reflect light evenly throughout the room.

In a mid-size bathroom, partition walls can be used to separate the hygienic zone and bathing areas.

All the lines in this bathroom are vertical or horizontal, providing visual unity throughout the space.

A single, minimalist decorative element gives this bathroom its own special style.

Bright colors reflect light and make a room seem larger. Dark colors absorb light and make spaces of all sizes seem smaller.

Architect: Mark Guard
Photography: © John Bennett

Materials

The Best Materials

All the materials in your bathroom must be moisture-resistant, and ceramic and wood have long been the predominant choices. These days, designers are also experimenting with non-traditional materials including metal, concrete, stone, glass, fiberglass, and plastic.

Traditionally, bathroom cabinets are made of wood, a flexible material that adds a warm touch to any room. Some types of wood are known to work better in humid conditions than others, such as maple, oak, and cedar. Endangered tropical woods like teak, which were once common in bathrooms, are used less often today.

Marble bathroom countertops bring elegance to any bathroom, but it is both cool to the touch and somewhat difficult to combine with other materials. Granite is not recommended. When they are wet, granite floors are especially slippery.

Mosaics can be made from marble, stone, or ceramic tiles. They look wonderful in bathrooms, provided the level of craftsmanship is high. There is nothing more unattractive in a bathroom than poorly applied mortar overflowing the gaps between tiles.

Design: Giovanni Longo, Alessandro Palmarini, Igor Rebosio, Federico Spagnulo/Studio A Photography: © Andrea Martiradonna

Photography: © Jordi Sarrà

Design: Joan Bach Photography: © Jordi Miralles

Wood

Wood adds warmth to a room, and it can be fashioned into almost anything. Although it is very common in bathrooms, it is important to remember that not all types of wood are capable of withstanding both high humidity and direct contact with splashing water. In general, only woods with high oil content can be used without extensive treatment beforehand. Wood can also change in appearance over time. Antique-style wooden bathroom furnishings are a good decorative choice, but if you don't want your wood to look aged, be prepared for considerable care and conservation.

Although wood is chiefly used for bathroom cabinets and decorative details, it can also be used for partitions or exterior paneling for a bathtub or shower. Parquet floors are an attractive option, provided the right kind of wood is available. Many washstands are also made of wood. Wood should not be used on surfaces that are exposed to running water, and too much wood in a small bathroom can be monotonous. Wood is especially attractive when used as a contrasting element in combination with other materials. Light-colored wood paneled walls or parquet floors can be beautifully dramatic.

Design: Annie Stevens
Photography: © Jake Fitzjones/Red Cover

Photography: © Ken Hayden/Red Cover

Design: Anna Genero/Ivalo Photography: © Núria Fuentes, Ideal Standard

Design: Dry Design Photography: © Undine Pröhl

Architect: Lilia Konrad

Architect: Toni García Photography: © Ángel Luis Baltanás

Architect: Concept Consult Architectes Photography: © Pierre Boss

Architect: Joan Pons Forment Photography: © Eugeni Pons

Metal

Metal furnishings and finishes are increasingly popular options for bathrooms. Aluminum, iron, titanium, and other metals, while different from each other in many ways, are all prized for their shiny surface, resilience, and ability to hold heat. Lighter metals such as aluminum are the most commonly used.

Aluminum never rusts, making it ideal for moist bathroom environment; stainless steel shares this quality. Most other metals will oxidize if exposed to constant humidity, running water, or splashing. Remember that many metal furnishings, while certainly attractive, are not meant for use in a bathroom. Nearly every kind of bathroom furnishing is now available in metal as well as other materials, from the sink to the toilet seat. Creative use of metal in place of more traditional materials like wood brings a touch of modernity to any bathroom.

Design: Manuel Ocaña del Valle
Photography: © Alfonso Postigo

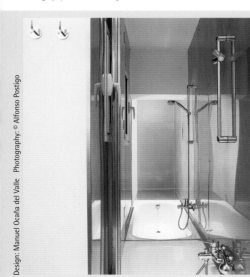

Design: Manuel Ocaña del Valle Photography: © Alfonso Postigo

Design: Manuel Ocaña del Valle Photography: © Alfonso Postigo

Architect: Augusto Le Monnier Interior design: Lorna Agustí & Natalia G. Novelles

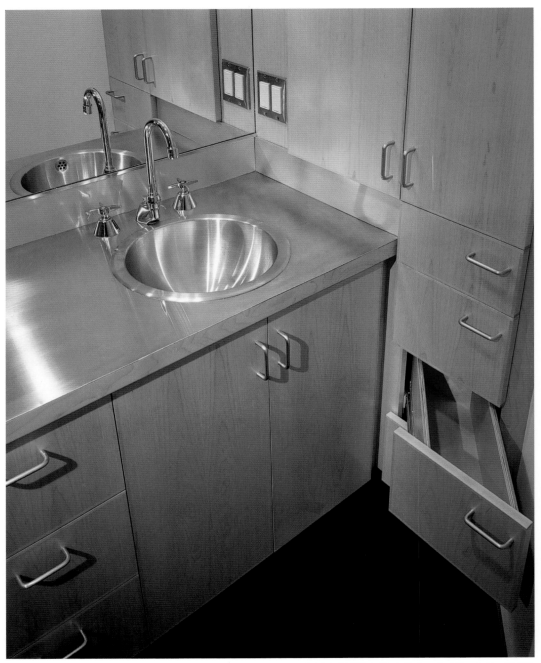

Architect: Eric Cobb Architects Photography: © Steve Keating, Eric Cobb

Architect: Messana O'Rorke Architects Photography: © Elizabeth Felicella

Glass

The use of glass—usually a smoked or tinted variety—while not uncommon in bathrooms, is usually limited to partitions and similar elements such as sliding cabinet doors. Glass is by far the best choice for physically separating one area from another in bathrooms large and small. When used to enclose a shower or bathtub, glass protects against splash water without blocking light. Depending on the quality of your water, glass that frequently comes in contact with water may need considerable care to avoid water spotting.

The more significant downside of glass is its cost: it is expensive compared to many other materials with similar qualities, including plastics. It is, however, far superior. Moisture does not affect glass and mold does not grow on it, making it very nearly the perfect bathroom material. The most expensive variety is industrial-strength molded glass, which is manufactured by a process similar to the production of fine crystal. Glass panels can be thin or thick. Due to their breakability, these may not be the best choice for households with small children. New applications include glass sinks, which give your bathroom an air of extravagance, but also of lightness and grace.

Architect: Daniele Claudio Taddei Photography: © Bruno Helbling/Zapaimages

Architect: Slade Architecture Photography: © Jordi Miralles

Architect: Anima Photography: © Paúl Rivera/Arch Photo

Concrete

While concrete is an exceptional building material, it is not extensively used in bathrooms. Concrete is a mixture of binding materials, sand, water, and fine gravel that, when dry, is stable and rock-hard. In bathrooms, it is often used as a surfacing material for walls and floors. In the 1920s, the use of concrete in interior design increased when modern architects began promoting its use as the rational expression of an industrialized society. The concrete used in designer interiors is generally a very fine variety. In bathrooms, concrete bathtubs or sinks are on the rise.

Concrete gives a bathroom a modern, avant-garde aesthetic that could not be in greater contrast with traditional design. It works best with minimalist or industrial fixtures, or as part of an apartment or house in which the overall design concept rejects excessive decoration and extraneous furnishings. Concrete is simple and straightforward, and makes the greatest impact unadorned. The unique qualities of concrete as well as its indestructibility, suggest that its use in bathrooms will continue to increase.

Photography: © Reto Guntli/Red Cover

Photography: © Henry Wilson/Red Cover

Architect: Avatar Architettura Photography: © Pietro Chelli

Photography: © Yael Pincus

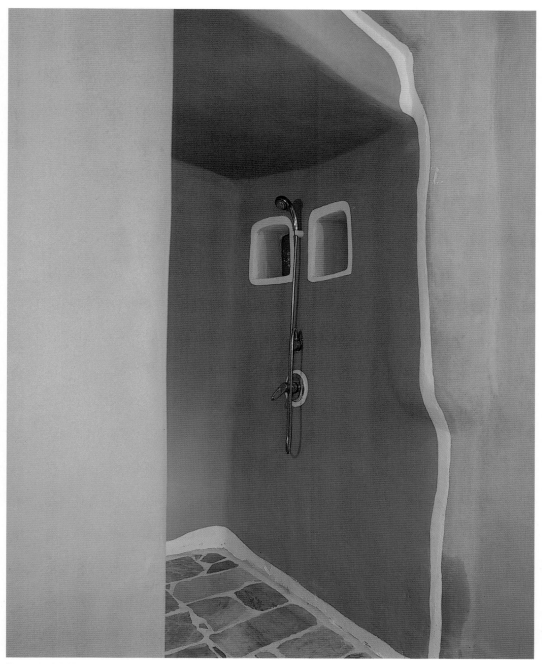

Photography: © Yael Pincus

Tile

Bathroom tile can be made out of marble, glazed or unglazed ceramic, glass, crystal, stone, or any other waterproof material and assembled in a mosaic. The word "mosaic" comes from the ancient Greek word *mousa*, which in Latin became *musivus*, which is related to the word "muse." The muses were the goddesses of the arts—proof that the ancients prized mosaics very highly indeed. No chemicals are used in making tile. For the clay varieties, firing in a kiln at very high temperatures, perhaps with the addition of a glaze, are all that is required. As a result, bathroom tile is exceptionally resilient and able to withstand a wide range of temperatures and moisture conditions.

Bathroom tile can be laid in any number of ways, and is available in a nearly endless range of shapes, sizes, and colors. It is by far the most popular material for bathroom surfaces, although it is also one of the most expensive. Laying bathroom tile correctly requires expert craftsmanship. The right mix of mortar must be applied evenly so that it is not pressed out from between the tiles and mar their surface. Wall tiling is often laid from the floor to a maximum height of 6 feet (180 cm), with the remaining distance to the ceiling painted or plastered.

Design: Odile Veillon
Photography: © Hervé Abbadie

Design: Makoto Tanaka   Photography: © Makoto Tanaka

Design: Jonathan Clark   Photography: © Jan Baldwin/Narratives

Architect: Caramel Architekten Photography: © Caramel Architekten

Architect: Caramel Architekten Photography: © Caramel Architekten

Design: Jonathan Clark Photography: © Jan Baldwin/Narratives

Architect: C. Matsuba/Tele-design Photography: © Ryota Atarashi

Architect: Slade Architecture Photography: © Jordi Miralles

Architect: White Arquitectos, White Design Photography: © Bert Leandersonn, Richard Lindor

Architect: Studio Del Portico Photography: © Andrea Martiradonna

Architect: Anima Photography: © Paúl Rivera/Arch Photo

Architect: Beriot, Bernardini & Gorini Photography: © Ángel Luis Baltanás

Marble and Ceramic

Marble is a crystalline form of limestone. It is extraordinarily hard and strong, but also non-porous and relatively easy to work. It is completely resistant to moisture. While this makes marble a good choice for your bathroom, it comes at a high price. It is also rather cold, both to the touch and visually. Marble works best in combination with warmer materials.

Ceramic is one of humankind's oldest manufactured materials, and it has many characteristics in common with marble. Ceramic is particularly resilient against heat and cold, and it is moisture resistant as well. The ceramic most commonly used in the hygienic zone is called stoneware, made of clay so dense that it is already completely waterproof before firing. Easy-cleaning ceramic surfaces lend your bathroom visual unity and fit particularly well with minimalist, straightforward designs. Ceramic tiles can be laid in almost any conceivable pattern in different colors, sizes, and shapes. Ceramic shares one disadvantage with marble as well: both materials can be slippery when wet.

Design: Silvia Rademakers, Virginia Palleres
Photography: © José Luis Hausmann

Design: Ruhl Walker Architects Photography: © Jordi Miralles

Photography: © José Luis Hausmann

Architect: David Boyle Photography: © Murray Fredericks

Architect: Marc Prosman Architecten Photography: © Christian Richters

The shower, bathtub, and sink are not separated by partitions, which saves a lot of space.

The large window brings bright natural light into the entire room. The mirror and light-colored smooth surfaces reflect the light, making the room seem spacious.

The oval bathtub is the focal point of this bathroom. The form is traditional, but has a modern look.

Faucets with a single spout are a good idea where space is limited.

The soap dispenser and shelf can be reached from both the shower and the bathtub.

Architect: David Boyle
Photography: © Murray Fredericks

Architects
and Designers